The Princ…

The Princess, sent… Revolutionary Government to live … tower in the middle of a garden in the middle of a wood in the middle of a field, with nothing beyond but steep cliffs and the great rolling waves of the Perilous Sea, grows up with only a cat (but a very remarkable cat) for companion, until finally a king comes to rescue her.

Among other books by E. Nesbit are:

The Railway Children
The Treasure Seekers
The Would-be-goods
Five Children and It
Septimus Septimusson
The Princess and the Hedgehog

The Princess & The Cat

E. Nesbit
Illustrated by Michael Pollard

A Grasshopper Book
Abelard-Schuman
in association with Richard Sadler
London

First published in this edition 1977 by
Abelard-Schuman Limited in association
with Richard Sadler

ISBN 0 200 72424 X (hardback)
ISBN 0 200 72425 8 (Paperback)

Abelard-Schuman Limited
A Member of the Blackie Group
450 Edgware Road
London W2

Printed in Great Britain
at The Pitman Press, Bath

The day when everything began to happen to the Princess began just like all her ordinary days. The sun was shining, the birds were singing, and the Princess jumped out of bed and ran into the nursery to let the mice out of the traps in the nursery cupboard. The traps were set every night with a little bit of cheese in each, and every morning nurse found that not a single trap had caught a single mouse. This was because the Princess always let them go. No one knew this except the Princess and, of course, the mice themselves. And the mice never forgot it.

Then came bath and breakfast, and then the Princess ran to the open window and threw out the crumbs to the birds that flew down fluttering and chirping into the marble terrace. Before lessons began she had an hour for playing in the garden. But she never began to play till she had been round to see if any rabbits or moles were caught in the traps the palace gardeners set. The gardeners were lazy, and seldom got to work before half-past eight, so she always had plenty of time for this.

Then came lessons with dear old Professor Ouatidontnoisuntwuthnoing, and then more play, and dinner, and needlework, and play again.

And now it was teatime.

"Eat up your bread-and-butter, your Highness," said nurse, "and then you shall have some nice plummy cake."

"I don't feel plum-cakey at all today, somehow," said the Princess. "I feel just exactly as if something was going to happen."

"Something's always happening," said nurse.

"Ah! But I mean something horrid," said the Princess. "I expect uncle's going to make some nasty new law about me. Last time it was: 'The Princess is only to wear a white frock on the first Sunday in the month.' He said it was economy, but I know it was only spite."

"You mustn't say that, dear," said nurse. "You know your rosy and bluey frocks are just as pretty as the white." But in her heart she agreed with the Princess Everilda.

The Princess's father and mother had died when she was quite little, and her uncle was Regent. Now, you will have noticed that there is something about uncles which makes it impossible for them to be good in fairy stories. So of course this uncle was bad, as bad as he could be, and everyone hated him.

In fact, though it was now, as I have said, everybody's teatime, nobody was making any tea: instead they were making a revolution. And just as the Princess was looking at the half-moon-shaped hole left by her first bite into her first piece of bread-and-butter, the good Professor burst into the nursery with his great grey wig all on one side, crying out in a very loud and very choky voice:

"The revolution! It's come at last. I *knew* the people would never stand that last tax on soap."

"The Princess!" said nurse, turning very pale.

"Yes, I know," said the Professor. "There's a boat on the canal, blue sails with gold letters 'P.P.'–Pupil of the Professor. It's waiting. You go down there at once. I'll take the Princess out down the back stairs."

He caught the Princess by her pink bread-and-buttery hand, and dragged her away.

"Hurry, my dear," he panted, "it's as much as your life is worth to delay a minute."

But he himself delayed quite three minutes, and that was one minute too long. He had just run into the palace library for the manuscript of his life's work, *Everything Easily Explained*, when the revolutionary crowd burst in, shouting "Liberty and Soap!" and

caught him. They did not see the Princess Everilda, because he had just time, when he heard them coming, to throw a red and green crochet antimacassar over her, and to hide her behind an armchair.

"When they've taken me away, go down the back stairs, and try to find the boat," he whispered, just before they came and took him away.

And then Everilda was left alone. When everything was quiet, she said to herself: "Now, you mustn't cry; you must do as you're told." And she went down the palace back-stairs, and out through the palace kitchen into the street.

She had never set foot in the streets before, but she had been driven through them in a coach with four white horses, and she knew the way to the canal.

The canal boat with the blue sails was waiting, and she would have got to it safely enough, but she heard a rattling sound, and when she looked she saw two boys tying an old rusty kettle to a cat's tail.

"You horrid boys!" she said, "let poor pussy alone."

"Not us," said the boys.

Everilda instantly slapped them both, and they were so surprised that they let the cat go. It scuttled and scurried off, and so did the Princess. The boys threw stones after her and also after the cat, but fortunately they were both very bad shots and nobody was hit.

Even then the Princess would have got safely away, but she saw a boy sitting on a doorstep crying. So she stopped to ask what was the matter.

"I'm hungry," said the boy, "and father and mother are dead, and my uncle beat me, so I'm running away–"

"Oh," said the Princess, "so am I. What fun! And I've got a horrid uncle, too. You come with me, and we'll find my nurse. *She's* running away, too. Make haste, or it'll be too late."

But when they got to the corner, it *was* too late.

The revolutionary crowd caught

them; they shouted "Liberty and Soap!" and they sent the boy to the workhouse, and they put the Princess in prison; and a good many of them wanted to cut off her pretty little head then and there, because they thought she would be sure to grow up horrid like her uncle the Regent.

But all the people who had ever been inside the palace said what a nice little girl the Princess really was, and wouldn't hear of cutting off her darling head. So at last it was decided to get rid of her by enchantment, and the Head Magician to the Provisional Revolutionary Government was sent for.

"Certainly, citizens," he said, "I'll put her in a tower on the

Forlorn Island, in the middle of the Perilous Sea—a nice strong tower, with only one way out."

"That's one too many. There's not to be *any* way out," said the people.

"Well, there's a way out of everything, you know," said the Magician timidly—he was trembling for his own head—"but it's fifty thousand millions to one against her ever finding it."

So they had to be content with that, and they fetched Everilda out of her prison; and the Magician took her hand and called his carriage, which was an invention of his own—half dragon, and half motor-car, and half flying-machine—so that it was a carriage and a half, and

came when it was called, tame as any pet dog.

He lifted Everilda in, and said "Gee up!" to his patent carriage, and the intelligent creature geed up right into the air and flew away. The Princess shut her eyes tight, and tried not to scream. She succeeded.

When the Magician's carriage got to the place where it knew it ought to stop, it did stop, and tumbled Everilda out on to a hard floor, and went back to its master, who patted it, and gave it a good feed of oil, and fire, and water, and petroleum spirit.

The Princess opened her eyes as the sound of the rattling dragon wings died away. She was alone—quite alone. "I won't stay here," said Everilda. "I'll run away again."

She ran to the edge of the tower and looked down. The tower was in the middle of a garden, and the garden was in the middle of a wood, and the wood was in the middle of a field, and after the field there was nothing more at all except steep cliffs and the great rolling, raging waves of the Perilous Sea.

"There's no way to run away by," she said; and then she remembered that even if she ran away, there was no nowhere to run to, because the people had taken her palace away from her, and the palace was the only home she had ever had—and where her nurse was goodness only knew.

"So I suppose I've got to live here till someone fetches me," she said, and stopped crying, like a brave King's daughter as she was.

"I'll explore," said Everilda all alone. "That will be fun." She said it bravely, and really it was more fun than she expected. The tower

had only one room on each floor. The top floor was Everilda's bedroom; she knew that by her gold-backed brushes and things with "E.P." on them that lay on the toilet-table. The next floor was a sitting-room, and the next a dining-room, and the last of all was a kitchen, with rows of bright pots and pans, and everything that a cook can possibly want.

"Now I can play at cooking," said the Princess. "I've always wanted to do that. If only there was something to cook!"

She looked in the cupboards, and there were lots of canisters and jars with rice, and flour, and beans, and peas, and lentils, and macaroni, and currants, and raisins, and candied peel, and sugar, and sago, and cinnamon. She ate a whole lump of candied citron, and enjoyed it very much.

"I shan't starve, anyway," she said. "But oh! of course, I shall soon eat up all these things, and then—"

In her agitation she dropped the jar; it did not break, but all the candied peel rolled away into corners and under tables. Yet when she picked the jar up it was as full as ever.

"Oh, hooray!" cried Everilda, who had once heard a sentry use that low expression, "of course it's a magic tower, and everything is magic in it. The jars will always be full."

The fire was laid, so she lighted it and boiled some rice, but it stuck to the pot and got burned—you know how nasty burned rice is—and the macaroni she tried to cook would not get soft. So she went out into the garden, and had a very much nicer dinner than she could ever have cooked. Instead of meat she had apples, and instead of vegetables she had plums, and she had peaches instead of pudding.

There were rows and rows of beautiful books in the sitting-room, and she read a little, and wrote a long letter to nurse, in case anyone ever came who knew nurse's address and would post it for her. And then she had a nectarine-and-mulberry tea.

By this time the sun was sinking all red and splendid beyond the dark waters of the Perilous Sea, and Everilda sat down on the window seat to watch it.

I shall not tell you whether she cried at all then. Perhaps you would have cried just a little if you had been in her place.

"Oh dear! oh dear! oh dear!" she said, sniffing slightly. (Perhaps she had a cold.) "There's nobody to tuck me up in bed–nobody at all."

And just as she said it something fat and furry flew between her and the sunset. It hovered clumsily a moment, and then swooped in at the window.

"Oh!" cried the Princess, very much frightened indeed.

"Don't you know me?" said the stout furry creature, folding its wings. "I'm the cat you saved from the indignity of a rusty kettle in connection with my honourable tail."

"But that cat hadn't got wings," said Everilda, "and you're much bigger than it, and it couldn't talk."

"How do you know it couldn't talk," said the Cat, "did you ask it?"

"No," said the Princess.

"Well, then!" said the Cat. "And as for wings, I needn't wear them if you'd rather I didn't."

The Cat took off her wings, rolled them neatly up, like your father rolls his umbrella, tied them round with a piece of string, and put them in the left-hand corner drawer in the bureau.

"That's better," said Everilda.

"And as for size," said the Cat, "if I stayed ordinary cat-size I shouldn't be any use to you. And I've come to be cook, companion, housemaid, nurse, professor, and everything else, so—"

"Oh, don't," said the Princess—"*don't* get any bigger."

For while she was speaking the Cat had been growing steadily, and she was now about the size of a large leopard.

"Certainly not," said the Cat obligingly. "I'll stop at once."

"I suppose," said the Princess timidly, "that you're magic?"

"Of course," said the Cat. "Everything is, here. Don't you be afraid of me, now! Come along, my pet, time for bed."

Everilda jumped, for the voice was the voice of her nurse; but it was also the voice of the Cat.

"Oh!" cried the Princess, throwing her arms round the cat's large furry neck, "I'm not afraid of *any*

thing when you speak like that."

So, after all, she had someone to tuck her up in bed. The Cat did it with large, soft, furry, clever paws, and in two minutes Everilda was fast asleep.

And now began the long, lonely, but all the same quite happy time which the Princess and the Cat spent together on the Forlorn Island.

Everilda had lessons with the Cat—and then it was the Professor's voice that the Cat spoke with; and the two did the neat little housework of the tower together—and then the Cat's voice was like the voices of the palace housemaids. And they did the cooking and then the Cat's voice was the cook's voice. And they played games together—and then the voice of the Cat was like the voices of all sorts of merry children. It was impossible to be dull with a companion who changed so often.

"But who are you *really*?" the Princess used to ask.

And the Cat always answered:

"I give it up! Ask another!" as if the Princess had been playing at riddles.

"How is it our garden is always so tidy and full of nice fruit and vegetables?" the Princess asked once, when they had been on the island about a year.

"Oh," said the Cat, "didn't you know? The moles you used to let out of the traps do the digging, and

the birds you used to feed bring the seeds in their little beaks, and the mice you used to save from the palace mouse-traps do the weeding and raking with their sharp little teeth, and their fine, neat, needly claws."

"But how did they get here?" asked the Princess.

"The usual way—swimming and flying," said the Cat.

"But aren't the mice afraid of *you*?"

"Of me?" The great Cat drew herself up to her full height. "Anyone would think, to hear you, that I was a *common* cat." And she was really cross for nearly an hour.

That was the only approach to a quarrel that the two ever had.

Sometimes, at first, the Princess used to say:

"How long am I to stay here, pussy-nurse?"

And the Cat always said in nurse's voice:

"Till you're grown up, my dear."

And the years went by, and each year found the Princess more good, and clever, and beautiful. And at last she was quite grown up.

"Now," said the Cat briskly, "we must get to work. There's a Prince in a kingdom a long way off, and he's the only person who can get you off this island."

"Does he know?" asked Everilda.

"He knows about *you*, but he doesn't know that he's the person to find you, and he doesn't know where you are. So now every night I must fly away and whisper about you in his ear. He'll think it's dreams, but he believes in dreams; and he'll come in a grand ship with masts of gold and sails of silk, and carry my Pretty away and make a Queen of her."

"Shall I like that, pussy-nurse, do

you think?" asked the Princess.

And the Cat replied:

"Yes, very much indeed. But you wouldn't like it if it were any other King than this one, so it's just as well that it's quite impossible for it to *be* any other."

"How will he come?" asked the Princess.

"Didn't I tell you? In a ship, of course," said the Cat.

"Aren't the rocks dangerous?" asked the Princess.

"Oh, very," the Cat answered.

"Oh," said the Princess, and grew silent and thoughtful.

That night the Cat got out her rolled-up wings, and unrolled them, and brushed them, and fitted them on; then she lighted a large lamp and set it in the window that looked out on the Perilous Sea.

"That's the beacon to guide the King to you," she said.

"Won't it guide other ships here?" asked the Princess, "with perhaps the wrong Kings on board—the ones I shouldn't like being Queen with?"

"Very likely," said the Cat, "but it doesn't matter; they'd only be wrecked. Serve them right, coming after Princesses that don't want them."

"Oh," said Everilda.

The Cat spread her wings, and after one or two trial flights round the tower, she spread them very wide indeed, and flew away across

the black Perilous Sea, towards a little half moon that was standing on its head to show sailors that there would be foul weather.

The Princess leaned her elbows on the windowsill and looked out over the sea. Down below in the garden she could hear the kind moles digging industriously, and the good little mice weeding and raking with their sharp teeth and their fine needly claws. And far away against the low-hanging moon she saw the sails and masts of a ship.

"Oh," she cried, "I *can't!* It's sure not to be *his* ship. It mustn't be wrecked."

And she turned the lamp out. And then she cried a little, because perhaps after all it might be *his* ship, and he would pass by and never know.

Next night the Cat went out on another flying excursion, leaving the lamp lighted. And again the Princess could not bear to go to bed leaving a lamp burning that might lure honest Kings and brave mariners to shipwreck, so she put out the lamp and cried a little. And this happened for many, many, many nights.

When the Cat swept the room of a morning she used to wonder where all the pearls came from that she found lying all about the floor. But it was a magic place, and one soon ceased to wonder much about anything. She never guessed that the pearls were the tears the Prin-

cess shed when she had put out the lamp, and seen ship after ship that perhaps carried her own King go sailing safely and ignorantly by, no one on board guessing that on that rock was a pretty, dear Princess waiting to be rescued—*the* Princess, the only Princess that that King would be happy and glad to have for his Queen.

And the years went on and on. Every night the Cat lighted the lamp and flew away to whisper dreams into the ears of the only King who could rescue the Princess, and every night the Princess put out the lamp and cried in the dark. And every morning the Cat swept up a dustpan full of pearls that were Everilda's tears. And again and again the King would fit out a vessel and sail the seas, and look in vain for the bright light that he had dreamed should guide him to his Princess.

The Cat was a good deal vexed; she could not understand how any

King could be so stupid. She always stayed out all night. She used to go and see her friends after she had done whispering dreams to the King, and only got home in time to light the fire for breakfast, so she never knew how the Princess put out the lamp every night, and cried in the dark.

The years went by and went by, and the Princess grew old and grey, for she had never had the heart to leave the lamp alight, for fear that some poor mariners who were not her King should be drawn by the lamp to those cruel rocks and wrecked on them, for of course it wouldn't and couldn't be the poor mariners' fault that they didn't happen to be the one and only King who could land safely on the Forlorn Island.

And when the Princess was quite old, and the tear pearls that had been swept up by the Cat filled seven big chests in the back-kitchen, the Princess fell ill.

"I think I am going to die," she said to the Cat, "and I am not really at all sorry except for you. I think you'll miss me. Tell me now–it's almost all over–who are you, really?"

"I give it up," said the Cat as usual. "Ask another."

But the Princess asked nothing more. She lay on her bed in her white gown and waited for death, for she was very tired of being alive. Only she said:

"Put out that lamp in the window; it hurts my eyes."

For even then she thought of the poor men whose ships might be wrecked just because they didn't happen to be the one and only King with whom she could be happy.

So the Cat took the lamp away, but she did not put it out; she set it in the window of the parlour, and its light shone out over the black waters of the Perilous Sea.

And that very night the one and only King—who in all these years had never ceased to follow the leading of the dreams the Cat whispered in his ear—came in the black darkness sailing over the Perilous Sea. And in the black darkness he saw at last the bright white light

that his dreams had promised, and he knew that where the light was his Princess was, and his heart leaped up, and he bade the helmsman steer for the light.

And for the light they steered. And because he was the only pos-

sible King to mate that Princess, the helmsman found the only possible passage among the rocks, and the ship anchored safely in a little quiet creek, and the King landed and went up to the door of the tower and knocked.

"Who's there?" said the Cat.

"Me," said the King, just as you or I might have done.

"You're late," said the Cat. "I'm afraid you've lost your chance."

"I took the first chance I got," said the King. "Let me in, and let me see her."

He had been so busy all these years trying to find the bright white light of his dreams that he had not noticed that his hair had gone grey long ago.

So the Cat let him in, and led him up the winding stairs to the room where the Princess, very quiet, lay on her white bed waiting for death to come, for she was very tired.

The old King stumbled across the

bar of moonlight on the floor, flung down a clanking wallet, and knelt by the bed in the deep shadow, saying:

"Oh, my dear own Princess, I have come at last."

"Is it really you?" she said, and gave him her hands in the shadow. "I hoped it was death's footstep I heard coming up the winding stair."

"Oh, did you hope for death," he cried, "while I was coming to you?"

"You were long in coming," said she, "and I am very tired."

"My beautiful dear Princess," he said, "you shall rest in my arms till you are not tired any more."

"My beautiful King," she said, "I am not tired any more now."

And then the Cat came in with the lamp, and they looked in each other's eyes.

Instead of the beautiful Princess of his dreams the King saw a white, withered woman whose piteous eyes met his in a look of longing love. The Princess saw a bent, white-haired man, but love was in his eyes.

"*I* don't mind."

"*I* don't mind."

They both spoke together. And both thought they spoke the truth. But the truth was that both were horribly disappointed.

"Yet, all the same," said the King to himself, "old and withered as she is, she is more to me than the

youngest and loveliest of all other Princesses."

"I don't care if he *is* grey," said the Princess to herself. "Whatever he is, he's the only possible one."

"Here's a pretty kettle of fish!" said the Cat. "Why on earth didn't you come before?"

"I came as soon as I could," said the King.

The Cat, walking about the room in an agitated way, kicked against the wallet the King had dropped.

"What's this?" she said crossly, rubbing her toes, for the wallet was hard, and she had hurt herself more than a little.

"Oh, that," said the King, "that's just the steel bolts and hammers and things that my re-

solves to find the Princess turned into when I failed and never did find her. I never could bear to throw them away; I had a sort of feeling that they might be good for something, since they hurt me so much when they came to me. I thought perhaps I could batter down the doors of the Princess's tower with them."

"They're good for something better than that," said the Cat joyously.

She went away, and the two heard her hammering away below. Presently she staggered in with a great basket of white powder, and emptied it on the floor; then she went away for more. The King helped her with the next basketful, and the next, and the next, and the next, and the next, and the next, for there were seven of them, and the heap of white powder stood up in the room as high as the King's middle.

"That's powder of pearls," said

the Cat proudly. "Now, tell me, have you been a good King?"

"I have tried to be," said the white-haired King. "I was a workhouse boy, and then I was apprenticed to a magician, who taught me how to make people happy. There was a revolution just at the time when I was put into the workhouse, and they had a Republic. And I worked my way up till they made me President."

"What became of the King in that revolution?"

"There wasn't a King, only a Regent. They had him taught a trade, and he worked for his living. It was the worst punishment they could invent for him. There was a Princess, too, but she was hidden by a magician. I saw her once when she was trying to run away. She asked me to run too—to her nurse—"

Here his eyes met the Princess's.

"Oh," she said, "that was you, was it?"

"Oh," said he, "then that was you!"

And they looked long and lovingly in each other's faded eyes.

"Hurry up," said the Cat impatiently. "You were made President. And then—"

"Oh, why, then," said the King, "they thought it wouldn't be any more dangerous or expensive to have a King than a President, and prettier at State shows—ermine, crown, and sceptre, and all that—

prettier than frock-coat and spats. So I agreed."

"And do your people love you?" the Cat asked.

"I don't know," said the King simply. "I love them—"

As he spoke there came a flutter and flicker of many thousand wings at the closed casement. The Cat threw the window wide, and in swarmed a countless crowd of white pigeons.

"These are the blessings of your people," said the Cat.

The wings fluttered and flickered and fanned the heap of pearl dust on the floor till it burst into flame, and the flame rose up high and white and clear.

"Quick!" cried the Cat, "walk

through it. Lead her through."

The old King gave his hand to his poor faded love, and raised her from her couch, and together they passed through the clear fire made of her patience and self-sacrifice, his high resolve, and the blessings of his people. And they came out of that fire on the other side.

"Oh, love, how beautiful you are!" cried the King.

"Oh, my King, your face is the face of all my dreams!" cried the Princess.

And they put their arms round each other and cried for joy, because now they were both young and beautiful again.

The Cat cried for sympathy.

"And now we shall live happy

ever after," said the Princess, putting her other arm round the Cat. "Dear pussy-nurse, do tell me, now it's all over, who you really are."

"I give it up. Ask another," said the Cat.

But as she spoke she went herself through the fire, and on the other side came out—not one person, but eleven. She was, in fact, the Professor, the nurse, the palace butler, footman, housemaid, parlourmaid, between-maid, boots, scullion, boy in buttons, as well as the rescued cat—all rolled into one!

"But we only used one part of ourselves at a time," they all said with one voice, "and I hope we were useful."

"You were a darling," said the

Princess—"darlings, I mean. But who turned you all into exactly the pussy-nurse I wanted?"

"Oh, that was the Magician," said all the voices in unison. "He was your fairy-godfather, you know."

"What has become of him?" asked the Princess, clinging to her lover's arm.

"He's been asleep all this time. It was the condition, the only way he got leave to work the good magic for all of us," said the many voices that were one.

"Let's go and wake him," said the King.

So they all went. And when they woke the Magician, who was sleeping quietly in his own private room in the palace where the Princess had once lived, he sneezed seven times for pure joy, and then called for Welsh rabbit and baked Spanish onions for supper.

"For after all these years of starvation," he said, "I do really think I may for once take a liberty with my digestion."

So he had the supper he wanted; but the King and the Princess had roses and lilies and wedding-cake, because they were married that very evening.

And when you have passed through exactly the sort of fire those two had passed through, you can never be old, or ugly, or unhappy again, so those two are happy, and beautiful, and young to this very hour.